ALEX
KUSKOWSKI

A FUN AND CREATIVE INTRODUCTION TO FIBER ART

COOL

EMBROIDERY

for KIDS

**Checkerboard
Library**

An Imprint of Abdo Publishing
www.abdopublishing.com

VISIT US AT WWW.ABDOPUBLISHING.COM

Published by Abdo Publishing, a division of ABDO, PO Box 398166, Minneapolis, Minnesota 55439. Copyright © 2015 by Abdo Consulting Group, Inc. International copyrights reserved in all countries. No part of this book may be reproduced in any form without written permission from the publisher. Checkerboard Library™ is a trademark and logo of Abdo Publishing.

Printed in the United States of America, North Mankato, Minnesota
062014
092014

Design and Production: Anders Hanson, Mighty Media, Inc.
Series Editor: Liz Salzmann
Photo Credits: Anders Hanson, Shutterstock

The following manufacturers/names appearing in this book are trademarks: DMC®, Fiskars®, Iris®

Library of Congress Cataloging-in-Publication Data
Kuskowski, Alex., author.
  Cool embroidery for kids : a fun and creative introduction to fiber art / Alex Kuskowski.
    pages cm. -- (Cool fiber art)
  Audience: Ages 8-10.
  Includes bibliographical references and index.
  ISBN 978-1-62403-307-0 (alk. paper)
  1. Embroidery--Juvenile literature. I. Title.
  TT770.5.K87 2015
  746.44--dc23
                        2013043075

TO ADULT HELPERS

This is your chance to assist someone new to crafting! As children learn to craft they develop new skills, gain confidence, and make cool things. These activities are designed to help children learn how to make their own craft projects. Some activities may need more assistance than others. Be there to offer guidance when they need it. Encourage them to do as much as they can on their own. Be a cheerleader for their creativity.

Before getting started, remember to lay down ground rules for using the crafting tools and cleaning up. There should always be adult supervision when a child uses a sharp tool.

TABLE OF CONTENTS

Sew Cool

D iscover the world of embroidery! Embroidery is the art of decorating with needle and thread. It is more than 3,000 years old and it is still popular today. Embroidery is fun too!

With embroidery, you can **spiff up** clothes, pillows, or even bags. All it takes is a few stitches. You can combine them to make your own designs!

All you need to start are needles, embroidery floss, and something to decorate. This book will give you an **overview** of basic steps, terms, and **patterns**. Step-by-step instructions make learning a breeze. You'll love to show off the things you make. Just turn the page to get into embroidery!

❖ Tools ᴏꜰ ᴛʜᴇ Trade ❖

EMBROIDERY HOOP

Embroidery hoops stretch out the fabric you use. This gives you a flat, even surface to work on. Embroidery hoops come in many sizes. A 6-inch (15 cm) hoop is a good size to start with.

Fabric

Embroidery can be done on any fabric. Try **felt,** linen, or cotton. Some **patterns** suggest a certain kind of fabric. Be sure to follow the directions.

Almost all fabric has two sides, a front and back. The color or design on the front is brighter. The duller side is the back.

Embroidery Floss

Embroidery floss is a special kind of thread. It comes in many colors. It has six strands twisted together. You sometimes need to separate the strands and only use some of them.

Needles

Needles come in different sizes. The higher the number, the smaller the needle. Embroidery needles are numbered 1 though 12. **Chenille** and **tapestry** needles are numbered 18 through 26.

EMBROIDERY NEEDLES

CHENILLE NEEDLES

Patterns

Embroidery **patterns** come with directions. They list the types of thread, fabric, needles, and hoop needed for the project. There are tons of fun patterns to choose from!

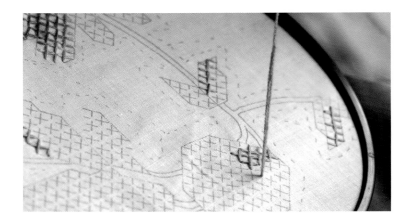

It's In the Bag

Keep a bag to hold your embroidery hoop, embroidery floss, fabric, and general craft supplies like the ones below!

BAG

BEADS AND
BUTTONS

MEASURING
TAPE

PEN AND PAPER

NEEDLES

GLUE

SAFETY
PINS

THREAD

SCISSORS

HOOP IT UP

PUT YOUR FABRIC
IN A HOOP!

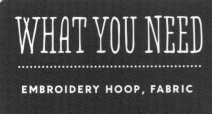

WHAT YOU NEED

EMBROIDERY HOOP, FABRIC

1 Loosen the screw on the embroidery hoop. Separate the two rings.

 2 Lay the fabric front side up over the inside ring. Center it over the ring.

 3 Press the outer ring over the inner ring. Squeeze the fabric between the rings.

 4 Make sure the fabric is flat. Tighten the screw.

 TIP The fabric must be at least 1 inch (2.5 cm) larger than the hoop on all sides.

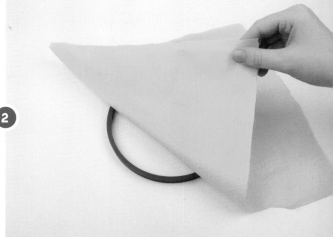

11

Basics

Needle Nose

How to thread a needle.

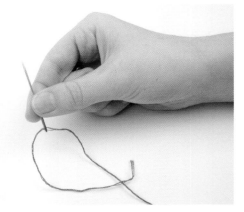

Cut a 20-inch (51 cm) length of floss. Tie a knot 3 inches (7.5 cm) from one end. Thread the other end through the needle. Pull it through 5 inches (13 cm).

Make Your First Stitch

This is the basis for every stitch!

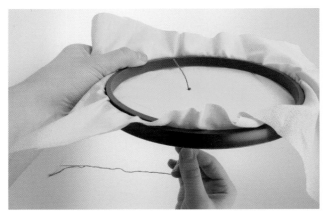

Push the needle through the fabric from back to front. Pull until the knot hits the back of the fabric.

Push the needle down through the fabric ¼ inch (.5 cm) away from where it came up. Pull it tight.

You just made one straight stitch!

FINISHING OFF

Keep your stitches from **unraveling**. When you finish a seam, knot the floss near the fabric. Cut off the extra thread.

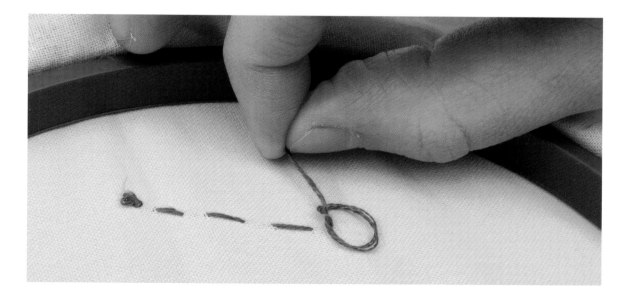

THE BACKSTITCH
(P. 15)

THE CROSS-STITCH
(P. 16)

THE SATIN STITCH
(P. 17)

STARTING UP

**GET GOING WITH
THESE DIRECTIONS!**

WHAT YOU NEED

**EMBROIDERY FLOSS,
EMBROIDERY NEEDLE,
FABRIC, EMBROIDERY HOOP**

THE BACKSTITCH

 Make one straight stitch. Move over ¼ inch (.5 cm). Push the needle up through the fabric to the front.

2 Move back to the end of the first stitch. Push the needle down right next to it.

3 Continue pushing the needle up through the fabric a stitch ahead. Push it back down at the end of the previous stitch.

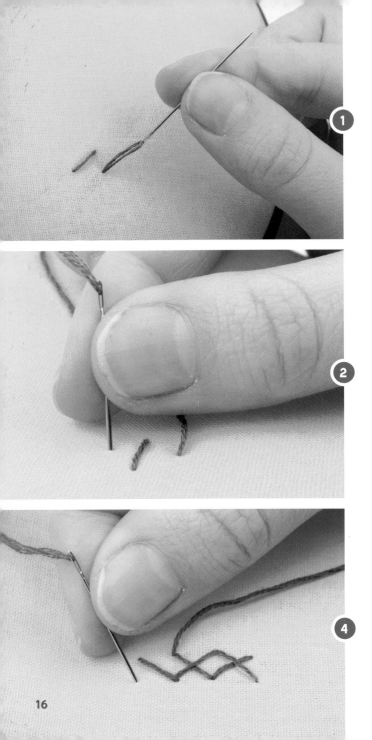

THE CROSS-STITCH

1. Make a straight stitch. Push the needle up next to the stitch ¼ inch (.5 cm) away.

2. Push the needle down on the other side of the stitch. Pull it tight. The two stitches should make an "x."

3. Push the needle up where the first stitch ended. Make a third stitch in the same direction as the second stitch. Come back up where the second stitch ended. Cross over the third stitch to make another "x."

4. Sew more cross-stitches. Try to make them in a straight line.

THE SATIN STITCH

 Make a straight stitch.

 Make another straight stitch right next to the first one. It should touch the first stitch.

Keep sewing stitches right next to each other. You can make them all the same size. Or you can make them different lengths to fill in a shape.

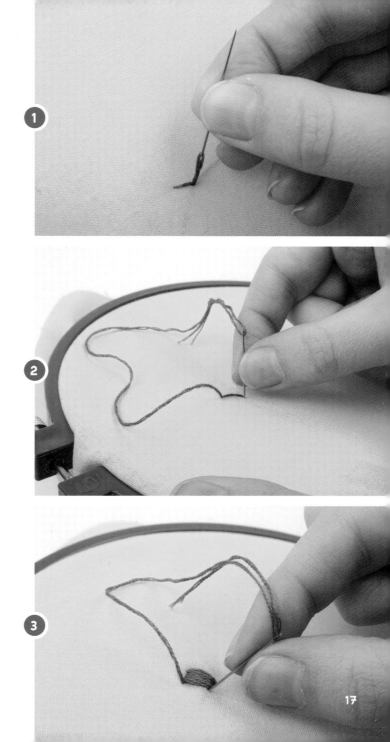

BLAST-OFF BOOKMARK

ROCKET INTO READING!

WHAT YOU NEED

PAPER, MARKER, MEASURING TAPE, HEAT TRANSFER PEN, FELT (BLUE AND WHITE), COTTON FABRIC, IRON, #5 EMBROIDERY NEEDLE, EMBROIDERY FLOSS (WHITE, TEAL, RED, ORANGE), SCISSORS

Draw a rectangle 2 inches (5 cm) wide and 7 inches (18 cm) long. Draw a spaceship inside the rectangle. Turn the paper over. Trace the lines with a heat transfer pen.

 Place the paper on blue **felt** with the marker side up. Cover it with cotton fabric. Set the iron on "cotton." Have an adult help you iron the drawing for 1 minute. Let it cool. Take off the fabric and paper.

 Thread the needle with three strands of white floss. Backstitch along the lines of the spaceship. Finish off. Backstitch along the spaceship's details with **teal** floss. Add flames with red and orange floss.

Cut out the rectangle ¼ inch (.5 cm) outside the lines. Cut a rectangle out of white felt. Make it the same size as the blue rectangle.

 Thread the needle with three strands of teal floss. Backstitch the rectangles together along the line. Finish off.

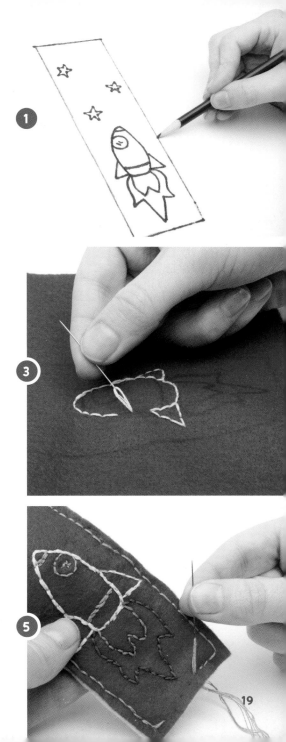

19

AWESOME ERASABLE NOTES

MAKE A NOTE TO USE OVER AND OVER!

WHAT YOU NEED

PENCIL, WHITE COTTON FABRIC, RULER, 6" (15 CM) EMBROIDERY HOOP, #5 EMBROIDERY NEEDLE, EMBROIDERY FLOSS (BLUE AND PINK), SCISSORS, CARDBOARD, DUCT TAPE, 4" X 6" (10 CM X 15 CM) FRAME WITH GLASS, DRY-ERASE MARKER

1 Use a pencil to draw a rectangle on the white fabric. Make it 4½ inches (11.5 cm) by 6½ inches (16.5 cm). Choose a short side to be the top edge. Measure 1½ inches (4 cm) down from the top edge. Draw a **horizontal** line. Draw horizontal lines every ½ inch (1.3 cm) after that. Stop at the bottom of the rectangle. Measure 1 inch (2.5 cm) in from the left edge. Draw a vertical line.

2 Put the fabric in the hoop. Center the rectangle. Tighten the hoop.

3 Thread the needle with three strands of blue floss. Backstitch the top horizontal line. Finish off. Backstitch all horizontal lines with blue. Finish off at the end of each line.

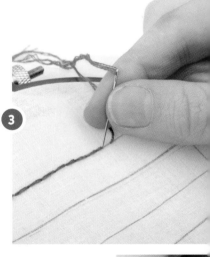

4 Backstitch the vertical line with three strands of pink. Finish off. Take the fabric out of the hoop. Cut out the rectangle ½ inch (1 cm) outside the lines.

5 Cut a piece of cardboard to fit into the frame. Center the fabric rectangle on the cardboard. Turn the cardboard over. Fold the sides of the fabric to the back. Tape in place. Put the cardboard in the frame. Write on the glass with the dry-erase marker.

OUT-OF-THIS-WORLD T-SHIRT

DON'T DELAY, APPLIQUÉ!

WHAT YOU NEED

MEASURING TAPE, SCISSORS, GREEN COTTON FABRIC, FUSIBLE WEBBING, MARKER, IRON, T-SHIRT, STRAIGHT PINS, 6" (15 CM) EMBROIDERY HOOP, #5 EMBROIDERY NEEDLE, EMBROIDERY FLOSS (GREEN AND BLACK), BLACK FELT, FABRIC GLUE

Cut a 4-inch (10 cm) square out of the green fabric. Cut a 4-inch (10 cm) square of fusible webbing. Fusible webbing has a shiny side and a flat side. Draw an alien on the flat side.

 Lay the green fabric down back side up. Put the webbing on top of the fabric with the drawing facing up. Set the iron on low. Have an adult help you iron the webbing to the fabric. Let it cool. Cut out the alien.

 Lay the alien on the T-shirt fabric side up. Use pins to hold it in place. Put the shirt in the hoop with the alien in the center.

Thread the needle with three strands of green floss. Bring it up through the edge of the alien. Satin stitch all around the edge of the alien. Finish off. Remove the pins.

Cut two eyes out of black **felt**. Glue them on. Let the glue dry. Stitch a mouth with three strands of black floss.

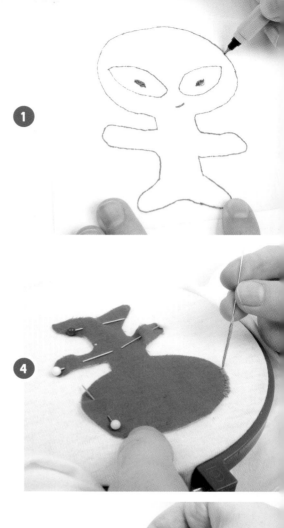

MARVELOUS MONOGRAM

BAG IT UP!

WHAT YOU NEED

CANVAS TOTE BAG, PENCIL, 6" (15 CM) EMBROIDERY HOOP, EMBROIDERY FLOSS (PINK AND GREEN), #18 CHENILLE NEEDLE, SCISSORS, FLAT BACK JEWELS, FABRIC GLUE

Draw your **initials** on the bag with a pencil. Put that side of the bag in the hoop. Make sure your initials are in the center.

 Thread the needle with six strands of pink floss. Bring the needle inside the bag. Push it up at the beginning of the first letter.

3 Backstitch the letter along the pencil line. Finish off at the end of each line in the letter. Backstitch the other letter with six strands of green. Finish off.

4 Glue on jewels for extra decoration.

25

SEW SWEET FRAME

WRAP A PICTURE UP WITH STITCHES!

1 Remove the glass and backing from the frame. Put the frame face down on the fabric. Line it up with the rows of holes in the fabric. Trace around the inside and outside of the frame.

 2 Put the fabric in the hoop. Center a corner of the frame in the hoop.

3 Thread each needle with a different color of floss. Use three strands of floss.

4 Pick one color. Backstitch along one edge of the frame outline. Use the holes to stitch a straight line. Go up through a hole, skip a hole, and go down through the next hole. Move the hoop as necessary to complete the row. Finish off.

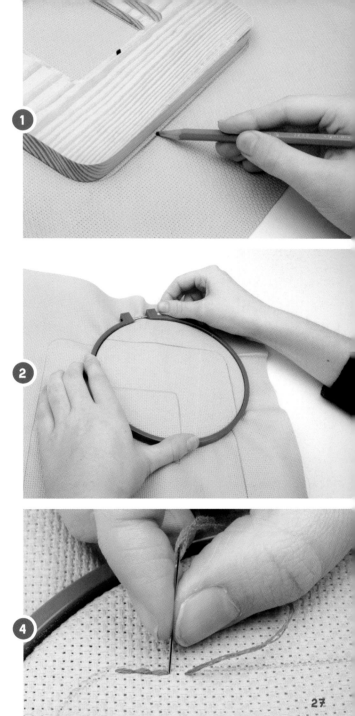

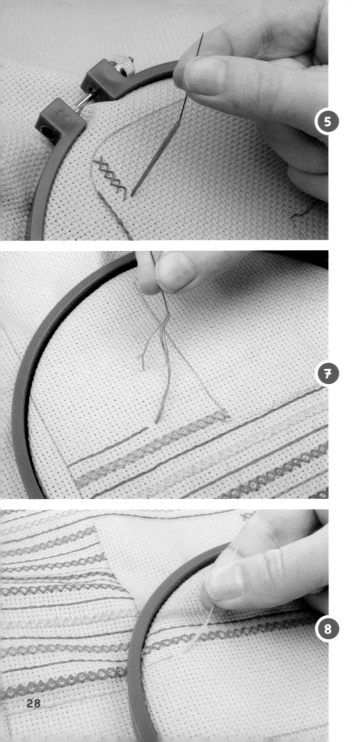

5 Pick another color. Cross-stitch a row ¼ inch (.5 cm) away from the first row. Finish off.

6 Continue stitching rows ¼ inch (.5 cm) apart. Change colors for each row. Alternate between cross-stitch and backstitch.

7 When you reach the middle of the frame, sew short rows on each side. Finish off after each short row.

8 Sew long rows again after you pass the middle of the frame. Keep sewing rows until you reach the edge of the frame outline.

Take the fabric out of the hoop. Cut out the frame. Leave a 1½-inch (4 cm) border around the inside and outside.

 Make **diagonal** cuts from the corners to the stitching. Make a cut on each outside and the inside corner of the frame.

 Lay the fabric frame face down. Lay the wooden frame face down on top. Put hot glue around the edges of the wooden frame. Fold the fabric up. Press the fabric to the frame with a craft stick. Let the glue dry. Put the glass, a picture, and the frame backing in the frame.

Keep Embroidering!

You can embroider almost anything! You can make cool stuff for yourself. Or make gifts for family and friends. There are tons of ways to use embroidery.

Explore craft and fabric stores. Check out books on embroidery at the library. Look up embroidery tips and projects online. Get inspired and create your own designs. Try dressing up old clothes with new stitches. Embroider a piece of art. It's all about using your creativity!

GLOSSARY

CHENILLE – a type of thick, fuzzy fabric.

DIAGONAL – from one corner of a square or rectangle to the opposite corner.

FELT – a soft, thick fabric.

HORIZONTAL – in the same direction as the ground, or side-to-side.

INITIAL – the first letter of a name.

OVERVIEW – the general idea or summary of something.

PATTERN – a sample or guide used to make something.

SPIFF UP – to make something look better.

TAPESTRY – a heavy, woven wall hanging with pictures or designs on it.

TEAL – a greenish blue color.

UNRAVEL – to come apart or to come undone.

WEB SITES

To learn more about fiber art, visit ABDO online at www.abdopublishing.com. Web sites about creative ways for kids to make fiber art are featured on our Book Links page. These links are routinely monitored and updated to provide the most current information available.

INDEX